A BLOODY MESS

Richard O'Brien was born in Peterborough in 1990, and has lived in Oxford and Nantes, France. He currently lives in Stratford-upon-Avon, where he is working on a PhD on the development of verse drama. His work has featured in *Poetry London, Magma, The Erotic Review, The Salt Book of Younger Poets* and *The Best British Poetry 2013*.

His first pamphlet, *your own devices*, was published by tall-lighthouse press in 2009, as part of the Pilot series for British and Irish poets under 30. A second pamphlet, *The Emmores*, was published in early 2014 by the Emma Press. He also writes a blog, *The Scallop-Shell*, dedicated to the close reading of contemporary poetry.

A
Bloody
Mess

RICHARD O'BRIEN

Ink Lines

First published in 2014 by Ink Lines
an imprint of Valley Press
Woodend, The Crescent, Scarborough, YO11 2PW
www.valleypressuk.com/inklines

First edition, first printing (November 2014)

ISBN: 978-1-908853-38-7

A CIP record for this book is available from the British Library.

Cover illustration by Estelle Morris

Printed and bound in Great Britain by
Imprint Digital, Upton Pyne, Exeter

Contents

Acknowledgements

Thanks are due to the editors of the following publications, in which some of these poems, or versions of these poems, first appeared: *The Erotic Review, Dead Ink, Poetry London, Ash, The Mays, Gulper Eel.*

'Four-Coned Ruth' and 'Plea to Future Philanthropists' were both broadcast on BBC Radio 3 as part of a performance in the BBC Proms Plus Late series.

Thanks also to David Tait, Dan Hitchens and Emma Wright for their editorial support and guidance.

'And that this place may thoroughly be thought
True paradise, I have the serpent brought.'

JOHN DONNE

Plea to Future Philanthropists

Dear Sir/Madam, permit me to dispense
with the delicate dance, the stately sidle-
up to the tablature of talent, bills and rent,
    the awkward pseudo-bridal
courtship of the caught-short and the idle,
and in its place submit a simple plea,
a free-from-frills request: invest in me.

But first, a test: let's get our money's worth.
I'd like a full account of who you are –
a tender-hearted thug, salt of the earth
or landed, under-handed, oiled from cars,
    a quaffer of champagne or caviar –
there are some caveats one ought to factor
in, when getting into bed with benefactors.

What, exactly, are we all together in?
If one of us has to be patronised
and it's the turn of capital to captain,
then it's prudent to ensure we won't capsize.
    Do any of the following apply:
consorting with consortiums, ex-cons,
funding hedges I can't prick my finger on,

or money sunning in some beach retreat
(*technical Virgin, undeclared in Kent*)?
With so much hanging in the balance-sheet
there is an ocean between 'broke' and 'bent' –
    so when all's said and spent
if you can outsource creativity
to your accountant, then you don't need me.

11

You *don't* need me. I'm ornament, gold-leaf,
no more essential than a mounted moose;
a taxidermist you can tax-relief,
Gift Aid against a gift with no clear use.
     What have you got to lose?
Preserve me: for a reasonable price
I'll preserve you. I'll bring my own supplies

if you've a spare wing you could take me under –
my jotting pad, a pack of Bics, my wits.
Keep me in tea; I'll try to show you wonders
beyond any public-private partnership,
     and by the Muse of Calculated Risk,
if you stand back – resist the urge to edit –
I'll do my best to bring us both some credit.

Projections

The night you told me 'love does not exist'
I slept with the projectionist.
Our hands unleashed trapped light

and let it spin. I couldn't face another night
with you debating how much past
is present in the present's aftermath.

'It doesn't have to mean something.'
She spooled, unspooled her tongue along my inside shin,
your negative. It's funny how it all winds up again.

My body was a planetarium. Her fingers were a laser pen.
The projectionist drinks Pabst and rolls her own
and has no message on her telephone.

Her thighs are piled high with celluloid.
At home you smoke and stare into the void,
change channels, read a book that tells you books do not
    exist.

I wake up next to the projectionist,
our mouths both pop-corn dry. The darkness hums with
    fiction.
I'm tired of you and all of your predictions.

She never has used the phrase 'the seventh art',
but she can tuck her toes behind her ears – look.
White mercury ignites your Bergman book,

the room lights up the way stained glass
was made to do if God ever came past
to thank the Best Boys, make the credits roll.

There is an empty socket in your soul
that paper couldn't stuff should it exist.
I told these things to the projectionist.

Ransom

I brought my heart to the car-park
    with a pistol to its jaw.
You brought a folded paper bag
    no bigger than before,
and each of us held out our hands
    as if it were rehearsed.

It seems to be a question of whoever blenches first.

I brought my heart to the interchange
    and hoped you'd join me soon
– alone in Didcot Parkway
    on a Tuesday afternoon –
and when I saw your squad of goons
    I panicked, I turned tail.

It seems to be a question of who has the weakest will.

So I sent my heart in a cavalcade
    behind the tinted glass
and you stood behind a road-block,
    warned me not to move too fast,
and held your fist up in the air,
    red dripping on your shoes.

It seems to be a question of who's got the most to lose.

    Entangled signals tight-rope walk
the wires between our chests,
    and yes, I'm looking down your top –
is that a Kevlar vest?

Can I hear a propeller blade?
Is this your getaway?

I've got a battered briefcase and I'm asking you to stay.

But you took my heart to the helipad
        and you bundled it inside
with a wad of cloth packed in its mouth
        and another round its eyes.
It seems to me, considering,
        we might want different things –

but I want you, and still, and that's what stings.

Campsite

No one goes camping forever.
There are logistics to consider: jobs,
the weather, unpaid debts, whatever else
uproots us from our lives like pegs
to leave a space the earth clots over.

Grass will heal more easily than skin,
but lover, let's pretend we're grass today.
Let's say I've rolled my sleeves up
and there's turf up to my thighs
and yours are leaves in rain.

Let's sign our names with twigs in mud:
a contract not to churn the soil,
disturb the homes of wildlife, or fuck things up
with any of the hundred kinds of carelessness
to which we have become accustomed. Yes,

we'll place our faith in the wilderness,
and if I shield your sun, you queer my pitch,
we'll take the risk. If it fails, it fails.
Our lips find trails, from underbrush to open glade;
leave traces that won't take too long to fade.

Single Men's Sculls

The remnants, the dispensible,
the lees, the dregs, the dull
in battered old dirigibles
with holes along the hull

come creaking to the shore
from which no traveller returns
with necks too weak for rollercoasters
sporting carpet burns.

The also-rans, the might-have-beens,
the castaways, the spares
cross over with the ferryman
in endless coxless pairs.

They stack themselves on podiums,
they pile up row-by-row,
awaiting an announcement
that they all already know.

The residue, the overspill,
the chancers with no chance,
the ones who didn't even get
to ask you to the dance;

the meek, the mild, the shy,
the underdogs with overbites,
the fumblers and the failures,
the unfailingly polite

with their dreams of vivid motion,
dripping sweat, exuding zest
become 'Still Life with Citrus'
on an art foundation desk

and the dispossessed, the malcontent,
the misled and unmissed –
the people come from miles around
to see it come to this.

They clear a space to sleep in
and lay out a bed for one
in the charnel-house of longing
– I preferred it on my own –

and when it's done, the done-for ones
head home alone, bereft;
but I will wait for you
until even the leftovers have left.

Moules

Splayed, like fat men
in ergonomic Swedish chairs –

each mussel's one clean break
tossed on the mass grave
of cracked-open shells.

They gesture, Hepburnesque, with *frites*,
these girls I met an hour ago.

It's Paris, and I'm nineteen years old.
Personal questions
make my glasses steam.

I pass the mustard, split
something in half. Inside

there is a small pink creature
alive and wriggling
ready to be swallowed whole.

More Sharks Than Ever Before

They told her that the world was her oyster –
salty, overpriced, and gone too soon,
and with the feeling she'd enjoyed it less
than everybody told her that she should.
A boisterous world, busy about her blood
with teeth on combs and brushes, bristles, tines.

They swim around her, dressed up to the nines –
the ones you call when someone needs an ambulance.
They split and slot their flippers into gloves.
They floss and smear concealer on their gills,
slick down their fins – they are advanced – but still
she hears the violins, and when they saw that note

as crisply as a blade across her throat
her heart goes pizzicato. With her arms exposed
in flimsy summer clothes, what if somebody reached
into the sky above South Kensington?
What if they squeezed that great big lemon sun?
Today's discovery: the fornicating slipper limpet

changes selves as easily as she forgets
to buy Danone, slips into last year's coat. It arcs its moulded
    back
as if to say: *Climb on, you don't know what you might become.*
The sharks have business cards and registered domains;
they know what ISAs are, and how to get red stains
out of a rug; buy shares, invest, insure, own table-cloths

and mugs that aren't for gin. The sharks convert their lofts.
Click, click, click, click – a stacking up of shelves
each one submerging and in time submerged.

The fear that, like that, she could just flip –
wake up a boy, or blonde, or blind, or twenty-six
and itching to be touched, not scratched, by somebody who
    slides

beside her, stubble-sleek, aerodynamic, glides
into her life and keeps on moving,
can't stop moving, drifting into nothing

as she clings, the top of a precarious pile
waiting in trench-light, changing all the while.

Purpled Thy Nail

Darwin never mentions jealousy.
He might have pitied it:

this tributary midge,
its small face smooshed

against your thigh –
how a discreeter buzz

could have withdrawn it
from life's sudden ledge.

Black capsule in which
you are now distilled,

returning for a second course:
it must be killed.

With one fell smash,
my hand becomes its hearse.

I cannot fault or blame
its aspirations;

it died for hunger, not for love,
though in the same location.

Its sacramental tapenade
beneath my nails on the train –

and was its sacrifice in vain?
That small, surprised, exhausted flood.

Come down, come down,
baptise me in your blood.

Bed Trick

'Just how neurotic do you have to be
to tie a knot in a valance?' you say,
or would if you were here. I turn away,
entangled in an ersatz tourniquet
tricked up from all six beds in which we've slept –
the one we've made, and lie in, doesn't count.

And maybe our *ur*-bed exists somewhere:
a pillow that would scarcely even sink
beneath my paranoia's horse-head weight;
fluff plucked from some Platonic eiderdown.
Tucked in the folds of time, it must be there:
a duvet that could bear the space you left.

But springs replace you; finger-jab at me,
disgruntled bouncers. Restless now, I think:
the world won't let you cover all your pain
with quilt and coverlet and counterpane;
it's morning somewhere. Well, be that as it may:
sleep deeply, love, and if you can, sleep late.

Some Marvellous Experience

I hope I have an accident today.
Nothing says sexy like a white IV:
'You'll see what's happened to my heart,' I'd say,
strung out on saline, clutching at *bons mots*.

Today I saw, out cycling, your ex-beau:
he dodged each curve with Donaghian grace,
a steady surgeon, braced against the wind.
He had no reason to recognise me.

If I could graft myself into his place,
or suture up the past like broken skin –
or if he could have had an accident,
the day you waited for him in that room...

The gears unmesh. He signals, dips and zooms;
recedes into unfocused ill-intent.

Distraction

Alone tonight, I dress up in your heartbreak.
I'm draped, ungainly, in its crumpled chiffon.
Picture a slick fish, gasping in a creel;
a boy caught in his mother's fishnet nylons.

In the place you drank, I order for your heartbreak:
'One of what she's having. Ice. Make it a long one.'
It's always my round, and no one's leaving early
(as I slur into the shoulder you once cried on.)

Now I wake up, cuffed together with your heartbreak
to find no one's come to bail us out of prison.
I dimly remember using our one phone-call.
When you asked me why, I couldn't give a reason.

Munch's Cock

is somewhere that it shouldn't be –
hooked on the hangings of a gallery wall,
strung up like lutefisk, grainily obscene.

It cannot be unseen. Consider it:
its flaccid grey 'What of it, sir?'
suspended like a broken wurlitzer.

Not quite a monster, Munch –
but then, who would be, underneath
the slow obstetric lights of new-born film?

No colour treatment, no Auguste Léon
to fluff it up. It cannot be retouched.
At once it disappoints and does too much;

makes all biography seem premature, limp
before the lactic acid fear of video.
You think about the cocks of history:

the wrestling scene in *Women in Love*,
Oliver Reed's clandestine tugs,
Fitzgerald in the Louvre sizing up.

We have lost that measureless humanity;
but we can see Munch's cock.
Shameless ambassador, predating Hitler's

single furious ball and Churchill in his trunks,
his whisky-sodden light artillery,
swimming in circles, drunk, directionless.

This will outlast them all: pinned up,
you proffer it like a *dagensrett*,
Oh Ed, red-eyed, relentless *selvportrett*.

Song of the Rose

a version of Maurice Fombeure

Oh, skittish-hearted, here it is,
the gift you asked me for:
the rose that lay between the lips
of a knight who went to war

when he came home behind the drums.
The drums are made of stone,
unlike the flower which comes
from love alone.

Like a flame whose jet falls
with a gold and purple flood
a rose's crimson petals
stain the sky with blood.

In the gardens of the past
the tender roses flower,
my friend entwines their stalks like grass
and plaits them in your hair;

in her mouth is the other
and its slow, sweet scent
rises above two lovers
now whose love is spent.

So Much Will Waste

Flat on my back in a Methodist chapel
I watch a plastic bag fill up with blood.
It's mine, and next to me is you, and yours
is filling half as fast and twice as red.
I hate to state the obvious, but baby,
we're already lying down, and when it's done
they'll toss them both together in a van;
we'll never see those pints of us again,
and they're no longer ours – other men

will share you, other women me, the secrets
of our hearts will whisper in the walls
of strangers' ears. So by comparison,
we've known each other years in this position,
since we know our bodies, young and strong,
were vetted good to go. It's all the same –
our tissues sank, we both filled in the forms,
and we could brush in arteries or veins
as close as passengers on rush-hour trains.

We'll breathe and bruise, it hasn't killed us yet;
the window closing when the platelets clot
is thin as plasters, fragile as the Tuc they hand you
in the blush of standing up. But this is not
the closest we could get to how it feels to swim
across a body like a foreign cell: forget the spinning
ceiling, then, let steel mosquitoes dive towards
the wrists of noble citizens. They'll do no harm
that we can't heal in one another's arms.

Mary Anning

Shin-deep in sand, your brother holds a skull.
You dust the beauty of a death as yet unnamed,
irregular, reveal a new age of the old. All hail
the salt-stained bone-girl. Georgian spume

subsides to something colder, less upholstered;
you're buried thirty years on, silted with laudanum.
You'd changed your church. Cliff-stark apostles
stood transfixed as men patched up your skeletons,

chipped out their names and wrote: 'extinct'.
The tide is turning, faster than you'd think,
or want. We're what's washed up. This is the old age of the
    new.
Forgive them, lord. They know not what they do.

Orpheus

None of the pluck
of the lion-taming lyre,
and none of the hands

that hush the hungry teeth
that chafe in the mouth –
no, none of the easy sleep.

And none of the songs
that stir the hearts of stones,
the skittish stilled,
the brooks running uphill.

More the lack of the will
to walk alone;
more the cricked neck,
the endless looking back.

Confessions of an Accidental Arsonist

How can I say what made me miss the embers
as I came to you, bun-heavy, fingers derelict with yeast?
Our sheets that night were warm as plague, a pie-crust,
and I felt your sleeping ribcage rise like loaves.
Outside, they didn't know our names, they turned
on spits of fitful sleep, but we were golden.
                    Slowly, love, we burned.

That night I dreamed I walked along the wharves.
The stars were crumbs, or fish too far away to catch;
the air played Chinese whispers, double-Dutch,
kissed me with salt it rubbed into my elbow-crooks
that stung like creaking timber, and a vast
sense of my littleness broke over me. I remember
                    the stories. Light in the east.

Our daughter reads incendiary books.
The wrinkles kneaded in her face are politics,
the new astrology. Her crossed eyes are a crucifix
and her virginity reminds me I will die.
I stroke her inky head. Her hair invents the match.
The rotten weight drowsing across the rooves
                    lifts its head like a latch.

Now something is rising in this half-baked city;
the morning light does a roaring trade, sold on
until every street is a red hand holding
another hand, the Thames a boiling butter-churn,
the houses dribbling new red humours. Look.
The future kindles cupolas and kilns and bricks.
                    We jump. Too many cooks

will spoil anything. That much we've learnt.
Blow on your fingers, shake off flour and slumber.
Now the news joyrides the wind. Unnumbered
wooden dotages collapse, choking, and the river heaves
a red-hot vomit. They are counting casualties.
My lungs breathe in all the ash of London, and it sticks.
       I breathe out, but it sticks to me.

Prince Henry's Autopsy

This is a knot in the Great Chain.
Lay out the Prince, and then what that entails;
unlace his chest. Fold back his red lapels
and hold a lantern up to his entrails.
This is a blot on the grand scheme.
This is a loss, in a big way.

This was a job for a big name.
You stand before the table and its weight,
lift up and turn each dead hand of the State.
Teaspoons of juleps in the fading light.
These are your hands in the dark paste.
That was the hope of a bright age.

This sets a new standard for 'bad day'.
The printers loose a liberty of black;
his liver inks a river through the tracts
and where the gall should be, a withered sack.
This is the Press at a march pace.
This is a rock and a hard place.

This is you, faced with a tough case.
Gisant on gules; his thighs, his balls, his tongue,
something else bloated, blemished, overstrung.
No protocol governs the work you've done.
These are the eyes in the cold face.
This is the blood in the blue veins.

This is a missed cue on the world stage.
Tip out the skull like a pudding bowl;
root, like a pig for truffles, for the soul
and come up empty-handed, harried, old.
This is a knot on the Great Chain.
This is a mess, in a big way.

Actaeon

It's tearing me apart – and not just now –
before, I mean, the skin and teeth.
It's had its fangs in me for weeks;
I wake up with my tongue bright wet with blood
and something savage in my skin.

Would you have done it if it had been him?
The man's more stag than me; that A-Team chest
is hairier than mine will ever be.
You'd keep him whole, you'd drop that sheet
and have them leave you locking horns –

but me, I pushed the curtain back and fawned
on you, your whiteness water-pearled;
I had no eyes for all your serving-girls
and soon I had no eyes, no guts, no heart,
I glutted them with longing burst when bitten.

That time you took my tongue from me, unbidden.
If I had it back I'd do it all again. Some days
I chew my arm off just for practice,
send you cards that say: you are invited to
The Donner Party. My place. 8pm. RSVP.

What I mean is, I would happily and knowingly
allow you to devour every inch of me,
or even just a pinch of me, to claw me limb from limb
and pincer me or water-board me, stick me
with my quills but stick with me. I'm only flesh;

a bloody mess you wash off, then zip up your dress.
Now I am the man with the flailing hands,
I am the man with the frothing hounds,
you are the girl with your thighs untanned,
I am the boy with the cloven hooves,

skittering loose as the landscape moves
and falling into the furious pack
because I was the boy who could not look back.
Delirious antlers explode from my head.
I am the artist and my hands are red.

Four-Coned Ruth

Ruth was a tetrachromat
       in a small town by the sea,
which meant she saw a colour more
       than her neighbours' eyes could see;

or rather, more than a colour more
       than the common red, blue, green –
she saw the shades those mixtures made
       and the secret shades between.

So: red for Ruth had a glint of green,
       green was a grade of red,
and yellow grew from the bluest blue
       like flowers from the dead.

If in every lie lay an anagram
       which assembled, spelt the truth –
that was the way the world conveyed
       its light to four-coned Ruth.

But Ruth kept quiet, mostly –
       in that small town by the sea
one didn't boast about the almost
       extra-sensory.

See, what was known was what was felt,
       and what was seen made sense,
and sense was shared. People were scared
       of Ruth. She made them tense.

By implication, all their lives
        they'd seen the rainbow wrong,
or not enough. If her cones were buds
        on wagging small-town tongues

water would taste like sparkling wine,
        sweet wine like dry vermouth;
you would be thirsty, fit to burst
        if you were four-coned Ruth.

Let's say she took a lover, Ruth,
        in that small town by the sea –
and for argument's sake, and to up the stakes,
        let's say that it was me –

and suppose her skin was as sensitive
        as her irises to light,
then twice as much. Dark doubles touch;
        we only met at night.

Then imagine a feeling, next to which
        the times all tension spilled
to a shiver so pure it verged on air
        would seem like a dentist's drill

to a patient without anaesthesia,
        turned in a rotten tooth –
let's say my body felt that way
        in the arms of four-coned Ruth.

Or so she'd tell me, when we met
        in that small town by the sea,
where the sky would spit, and us within it,
        iridescently.

But Ruth grew tired, eventually,
        of the limits of my view –
I guess we saw things differently,
        as lovers sometimes do,

and lasers can't correct all defects
        – trust me, friends, I've tried –
or even most; but come close.
        Closer. Look into my eyes:

if you believe, for confirmation,
        if you don't, for proof.
You'd see what's hid beneath these lids
        if you were four-coned Ruth.

Victorian Pornography

And looking out, like butterflies in glass
we want their eyes sad as we guess they were
when fucked in monochrome, pinned to the past
by more than frills, fabulous hats and hair
so sleek we might mistake it for our own
and, unaware the skin around it shrinks,
imagine it, in unmarked coffins, grown
thick in holy waves; or so we think.
We aren't prepared for this;
this buoyancy, this sense of play
that beckons more than any arse or tits,
surprising as the peep-show at Pompeii
where men could turn a key, lift up a hinge;
see secrets – close it – gone, as swift as wings.

Notes

'More Sharks Than Ever Before':

◉ The fornicating slipper limpet, known in Britain as the common slipper limpet, is a species of sea snail and protandrous hermaphrodite; born male, when a specimen of *Crepidula fornicata* settles on a limpet stack it can subsequently change sex and develop into a female.

'Munch's Cock':

◉ Auguste Léon (1857-1942) was a French photographer who worked with Albert Kahn on the 'Archives of the Planet' project in the 1910s and 20s: an ambitious scheme to document the world's cultures, using an early form of colour photography.

◉ During the filming of the famous 'naked wrestling' scene in *Women in Love* (1969), Oliver Reed is reported to have repeatedly manipulated his own genitals in breaks from shooting in order to match up to his co-star, Alan Bates.

◉ F. Scott Fitzgerald's paranoia about his own endowments is documented in Ernest Hemingway's *A Moveable Feast*; Hemingway takes his fellow writer to the Louvre Museum and suggests that Fitzgerald compare himself with the Greek statuary on display.

◉ In Norwegian, 'lutefisk' is a type of dried and salted fish, prepared with lye; a 'dagensrett' is a restaurant's daily special.

'Prince Henry's Autopsy':

◉ Henry Frederick Stuart (1594-1612) was the son of King James I and heir to the English and Scottish thrones. An ideal courtier with expectations of greatness, he died suddenly at the age of 18 from an attack of typhoid fever. Mourning literature proliferated upon his death, and his place in the succession was taken by the future Charles I.

'Actaeon':

◉ The Donner Party was a group of American pioneers who became stranded in the Sierra Nevada mountain range in the winter of 1846, some of whom eventually resorted to cannibalism in order to survive.